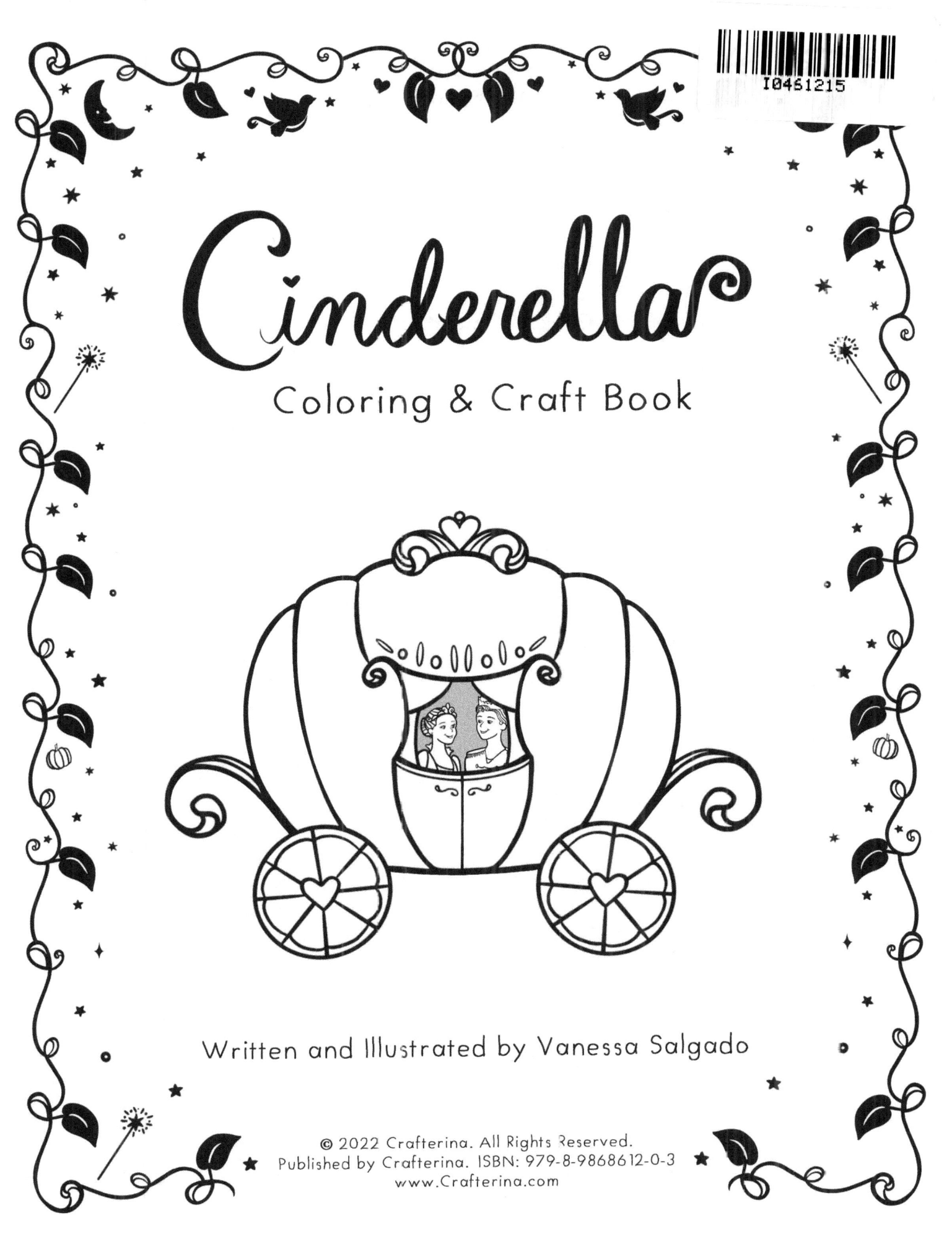

Cinderella

Coloring & Craft Book

Written and Illustrated by Vanessa Salgado

Published by Crafterina. ISBN: 979-8-9868612-0-3
www.Crafterina.com

I0461215

Cinderella

is a fairytale ballet with music by Sergei Prokofiev.

The ballet begins with Cinderella sweeping with her broom at home. All the while, her Stepmother and Stepsisters gleefully dance the day away as she cleans. Cinderella longs for a happier life filled with dancing.

Soon a telegram arrives with an invitation to attend the Prince's royal ball at the castle. Cinderella's stepfamily makes plans to attend without her. She hadn't ever been to a royal ball before and had always dreamed of one day dancing in a castle.

Later that night, she noticed a glow coming from the garden outside. To her surprise, it was her Fairy Godmother and the Fairies of the Four Seasons that wished to help. Using their magic wands they transformed a mouse and pumpkin into a horse and carriage! And with one more twirl, Cinderella had a ball gown! The magic would only last till midnight, so she had to hurry along to the ball.

The Prince greeted her upon arrival and they quickly became dancing friends. She was having so much fun, but knew the magic would only last till midnight. She decided to leave quickly and accidentally left her ballet slipper behind. The Prince found the shoe and set out to return it. Traveling all across the land he met many ballerinas, but none with the same slipper size. He was about to give up when he came across Cinderella's home. To his surprise, she had the matching slipper in her apron pocket. She tried them both on and did a perfect pirouette! He knew he had found his dance partner from the royal ball. Together they happily performed a beautiful dance for the kingdom.

Inside this book you'll find coloring pages and craft activities all related to the story! Enjoy crafting, moving, and learning at home with your family and friends!

For more dance and craft fun:

www.Crafterina.com

Cinderella

Stepmother

Stepsisters

www.Crafterina.com

Prince Charming

Fairy Godmother

Mouse

Pony

Pumpkin

Carriage

Cleaning Clothes

Ball Gown

Winter Fairy

Spring Fairy

www.Crafterina.com

Summer Fairy

Fall Fairy

Castle

Arriving at the Castle

www.Crafterina.com

The Royal Ball

Midnight

Prince

Her slipper falls off

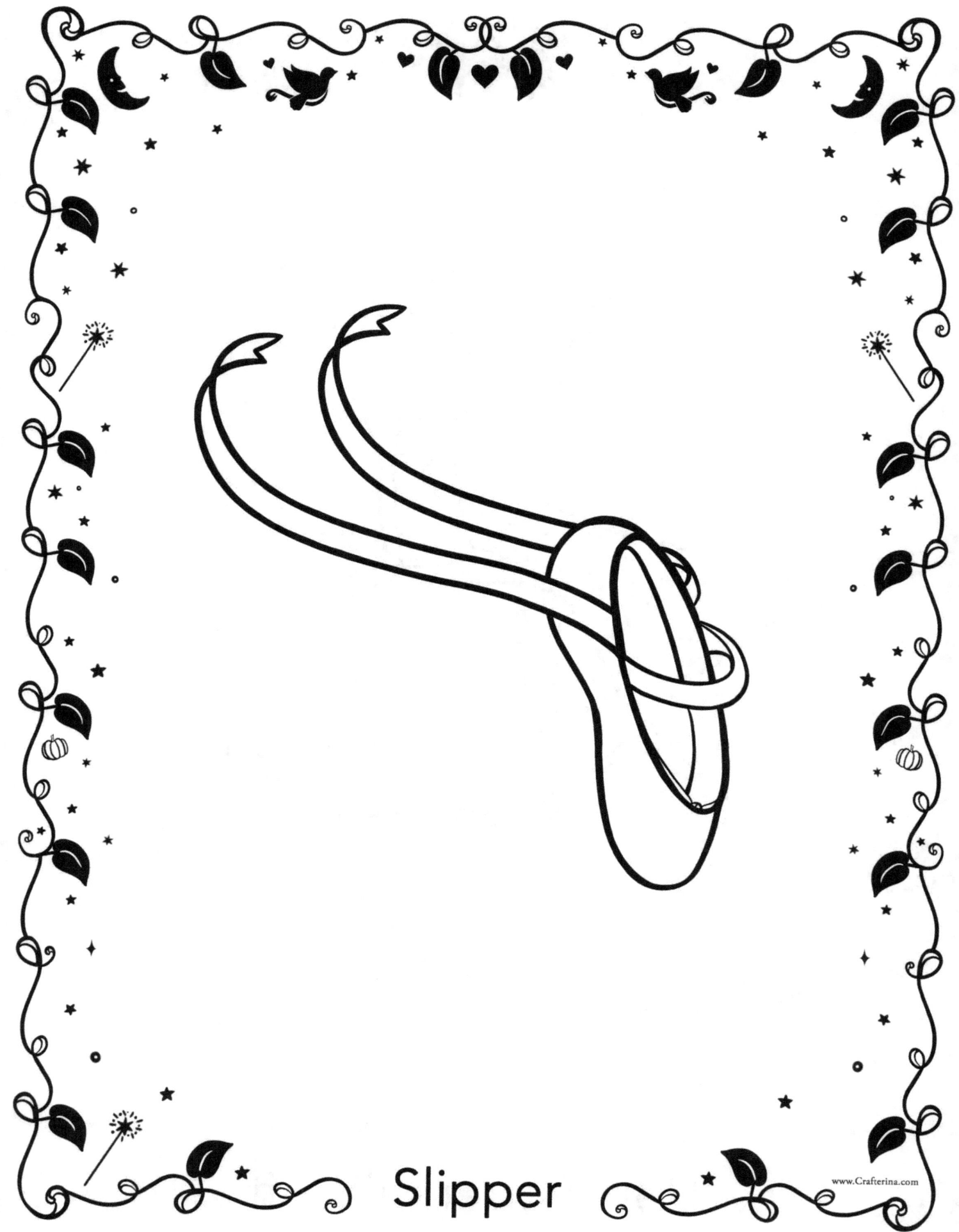

Slipper

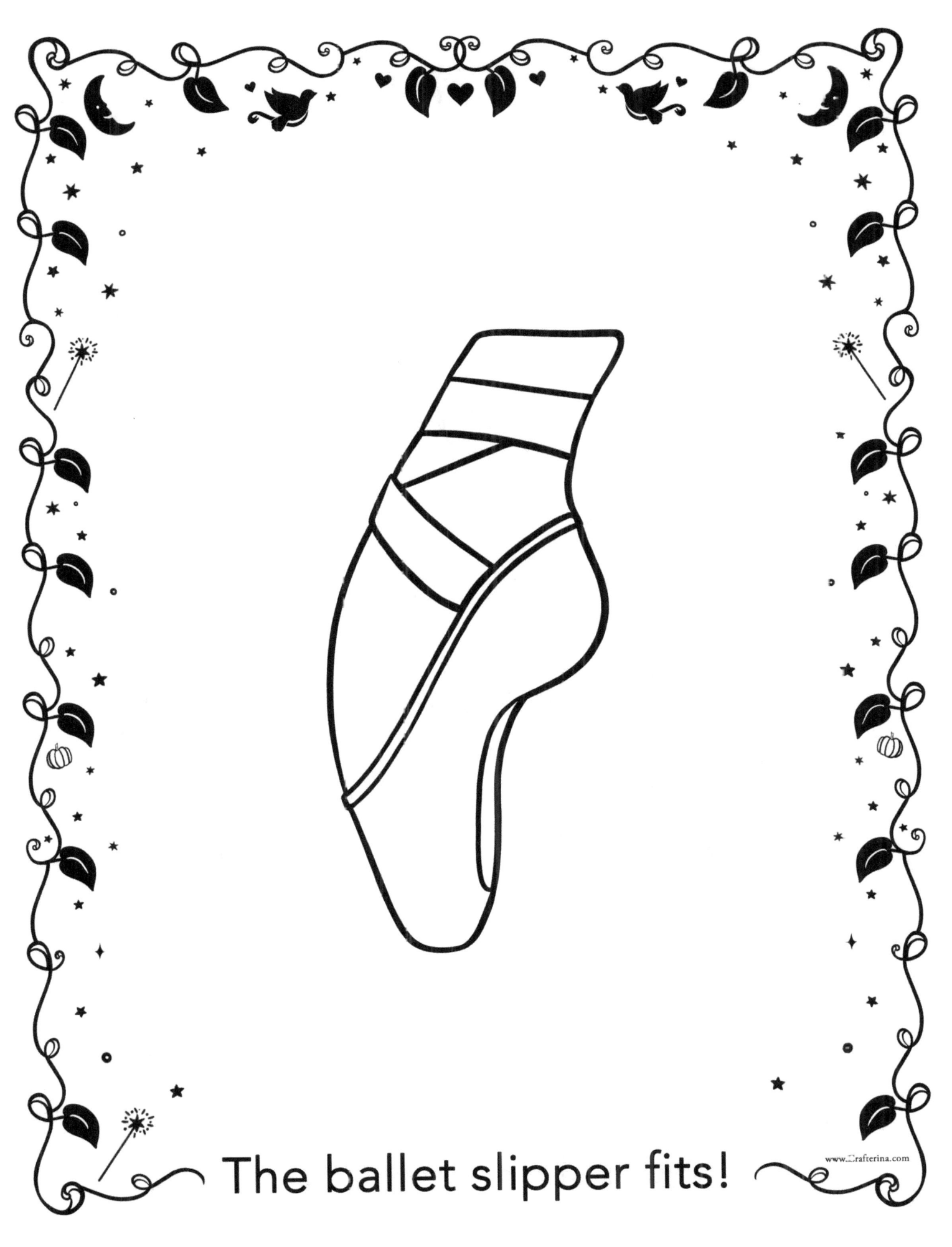

The ballet slipper fits!

The End

Prince Charming

Cinderella

Stepmother

Stepsisters

Cinderella Ballet Cast

www.Crafterina.com

Winter Fairy

Spring Fairy

Fairy Godmother

Summer Fairy

Fall Fairy

Cinderella Ballet Cast

www.Crafterina.com

Grand Jeté

Arabesque

Pirouette

Cinderella
Dance Steps

www.Crafterina.com

Can you twirl
in the wind
like a winter
snowflake?

Can you
grow
upwards
like a spring
flower?

Can you move
as calm as
a summer sunset?

Can you gently
move from
high to
low like an
autumn leaf?

Dance like the
Four Season Fairies

www.Crafterina.com

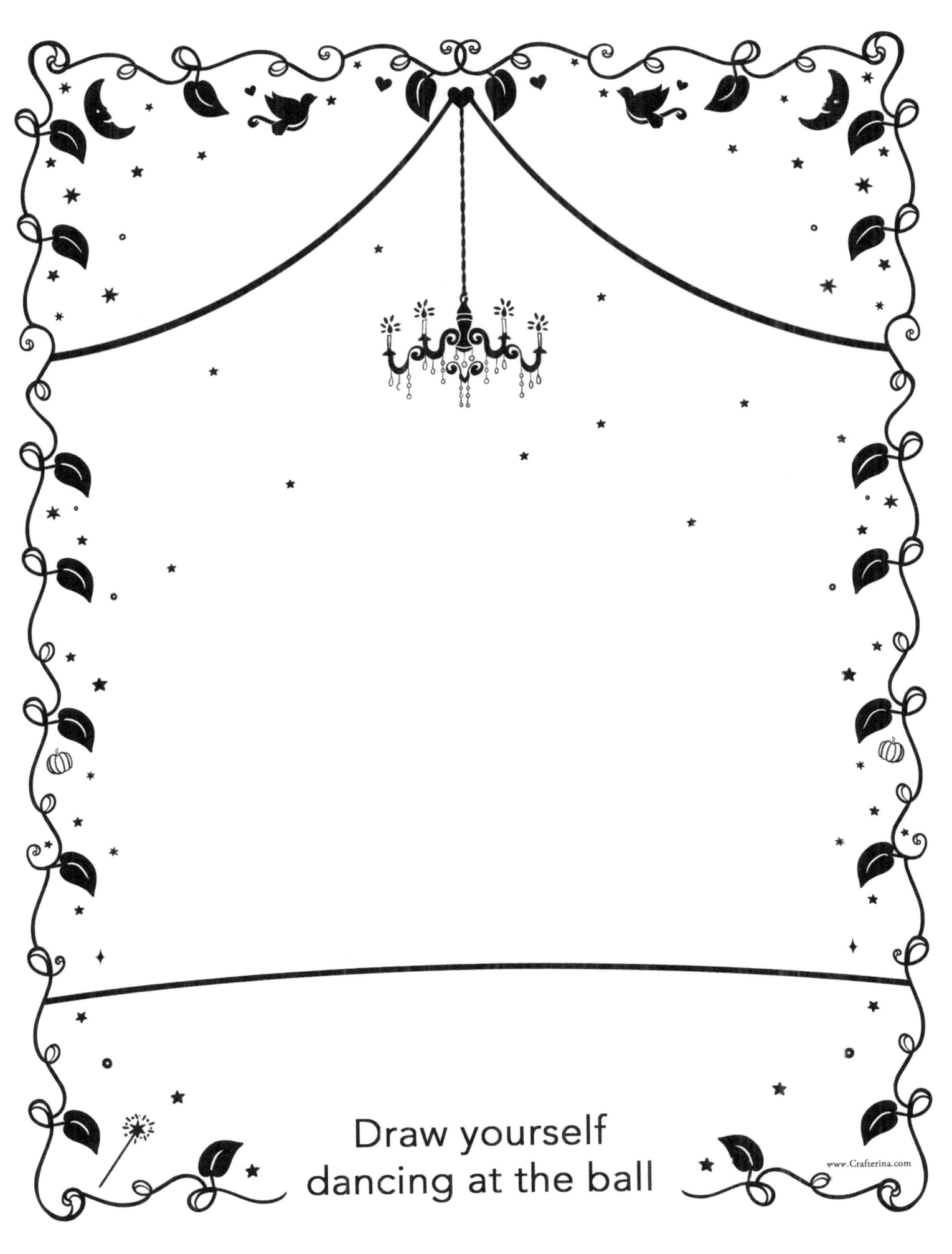

Draw yourself
dancing at the ball

www.Crafterina.com

Castle Clock

Write numbers 1 - 12 on the clock

Time Activity

Write the time of each clock below

__ o'clock

_ o'clock

_ o'clock

_ o'clock

Maze Activity
Help the Prince find Cinderella!

Start

Finish

Drawing Activity

Let's learn how to draw a pumpkin!

1. Draw a letter C

2. Draw a backwards letter C to the right

3. Draw one small curve to connect the bottom

4. Draw a small curve to connect top and add detail lines

5. Draw a stem

6. Draw two curves behind stem and add finishing touches! Draw leaves, vines, and swirls!

Use this area to draw your own!

Cinderella

Let's create crafts!

Safety Note For Parents: These crafts require parent supervision to create.
There are pieces to cut out and will require your help.
Have fun creating together!

Crown

Fairy Wand

Paper Doll

Castle

Cinderella

Paper Crown Craft

Directions:

1.  — Cut out crown template

2. Connect ends with glue or tape to make ring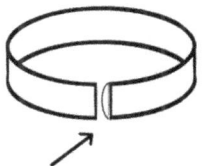

3. Time to celebrate!

www.Crafterina.com

Cinderella

Paper Castle Craft

Cinderella

Paper Castle Characters

Prince	Fairy Godmother	Cinderella

Directions:

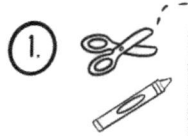

1. Color and cut out castle template

2. Cut along front door dotted line. Fold doors outward to open.

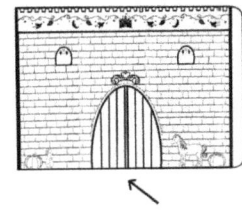

3. Use glue or tape on side tab to connect walls together to make 3D castle

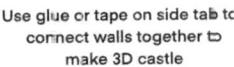

4. Cut out characters and fold in half
Fold ends outwards to create base
Use tape or glue to secure

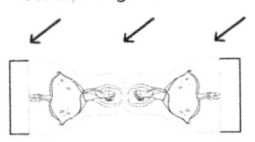

5. Bravo! You're finished!

www.Crafterina.com

Cinderella

Paper Wand Craft

Directions:

1.  - - - Cut out wand template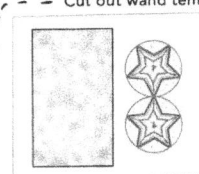

2. Roll paper to make wand handle
Use glue or tape to secure
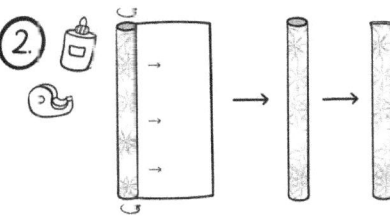
Flatten one end of the straw shape

3. Fold star shape in half
Glue wand in between and
press to secure shape

www.Crafterina.com

Cinderella

Paper Doll Craft

Cinderella

Paper Doll Craft

About the Author

Vanessa Salgado is a Professional Dancer, Educator and Illustrator.

She has taught many little dancers across Manhattan, concentrating primarily at the Joffrey Ballet School, School at STEPS on Broadway, and Alvin Ailey School. She has also worked as an Associate for the Education Department at New York City Center. Vanessa is a graduate of the Alvin Ailey/Fordham University BFA Program at Lincoln Center and holds a certification in Dance Education. Her work has been featured in Dance Teacher Magazine, Dance Spirit, Dance Informa, and METRO US Newspaper, among others.

Her earliest memories involve story time with her dad, creating with her mom after school, and attending weekend ballet class alongside her sister, Donna. Her interests in visual art blossomed in high school as she simultaneously trained for the professional dance world. As she transitioned from her college days into professional life, her incessant doodles and crafting have remained a source of wonder for all those around her.

For more information:
www.VanessaSalgado.com

About Crafterina®

Vanessa is also the creator of Crafterina® a series of dance education books and crafts for families. Designed to spark imagination and inspire movement at home, Crafterina® uniquely incorporates reading, creating and dancing in one. Through this interdisciplinary approach, Crafterina® playfully encourages empowerment and teaches youngsters they have the ability to make anything possible.

Inspire a lifelong love for learning in dance with the help of Crafterina®.

For more information, visit our website for books, crafts, and printables:

www.Crafterina.com

Crafterina

Find more from Crafterina by visiting:
www.Crafterina.com